THE WRIGHT STYLE

1995 ENGAGEMENT CALENDAR

THE WRIGHT STYLE

Natural colors and materials, stylized designs, strong geometrics, wide-open spaces, built-in furniture, brilliant siting—together, these features create the signature of Frank Lloyd Wright. No other architect in this century has left such a profound mark on how our buildings look: he indelibly changed the way we think about the spaces in which we live. □ In his long career, nothing challenged Wright (1867–1959) as much as designing the perfect house for contemporary living. He experimented always, moving from one mode to another to find the best expression of what he called organic architecture. Wright's earliest Prairie Style buildings presented clearly horizontal lines and sheltering roofs, conforming to the low midwestern landscapes of his birth. He tapped modern technology to build concrete textile-block houses in California in the 1920s and later "automatic" residences. Seeking a moderate-cost design for people of moderate means, Wright devised his sleek Usonian houses. Some of his work does not fit into any of these categories—among them the world-famous Fallingwater, boldly sited not near a waterfall but right over it. □ For each of his projects, Wright prepared an intricate composition of interrelated elements, much like the music he loved. He and his associates designed furnishings, art glass windows, textiles, accessories, landscaping, and even china. The result was an integrated, unified work of art to be used. In seven decades Wright received more than a thousand commissions, of which about half were built and some four hundred survive. Everything he created he imbued with his own personal sense of style.

HOLLYHOCK HOUSE (1917), HOLLYWOOD, CALIFORNIA. JAPANESE SCREENS, AN APPROVED WRIGHT FEATURE, ADD TO THE GOLDEN PALETTE OF THE LIVING ROOM.

DECEMBER ☐ JANUARY

MONDAY

26

TUESDAY

27

WEDNESDAY

28

THURSDAY

29

FRIDAY

30

SATURDAY

31

NEW YEAR'S DAY

● SUNDAY

1

ENNIS HOUSE (1923), LOS ANGELES. AN EXPERIMENT IN WRIGHT'S CONCRETE TEXTILE-BLOCK SYSTEM, THIS HOUSE REPRESENTS HIS LAST USE OF ART GLASS.

JANUARY

S	M	T	W	T	F	S	S	M	T	W	T	F	S	S	M	T	W	T	F	S	S	M	T	W	T	F	S	S	M	T
1	2	3	4	5	6	7	8	9	10	11	12	13	14	15	16	17	18	19	20	21	22	23	24	25	26	27	28	29	30	31

JANUARY

MONDAY

2

TUESDAY

3

WEDNESDAY

4

THURSDAY

5

FRIDAY

6

SATURDAY

7

SUNDAY ◑

8

TALIESIN (1911–59), SPRING GREEN, WISCONSIN. TO VIEW THE ROLLING RIVER VALLEY BELOW, A FORTY-FOOT-LONG "BIRDWALK" PROVIDES A PERFECT PERCH.

JANUARY

S	M	T	W	T	F	S	S	M	T	W	T	F	S	S	M	T	W	T	F	S	S	M	T	W	T	F	S	S	M	T
1	2	3	4	5	6	7	8	9	10	11	12	13	14	15	16	17	18	19	20	21	22	23	24	25	26	27	28	29	30	31

MONDAY

9

TUESDAY

10

WEDNESDAY

11

THURSDAY

12

FRIDAY

13

SATURDAY

14

MARTIN LUTHER KING, JR 'S BIRTHDAY

SUNDAY

15

TALIESIN (1911–59), SPRING GREEN, WISCONSIN. THE TALL-BACK SLATTED CHAIR RECALLS FURNITURE WRIGHT DESIGNED FOR HIS EARLY PRAIRIE HOUSES.

JANUARY

S	M	T	W	T	F	S	S	M	T	W	T	F	S	S	M	T	W	T	F	S	S	M	T	W	T	F	S	S	M	T
1	2	3	4	5	6	7	8	9	10	11	12	13	14	15	16	17	18	19	20	21	22	23	24	25	26	27	28	29	30	31

JANUARY

MONDAY ○   MARTIN LUTHER KING, JR S BIRTHDAY (OBSERVED)

16

TUESDAY

17

WEDNESDAY

18

THURSDAY

19

FRIDAY

20

SATURDAY

21

SUNDAY

22

HELLER HOUSE (1896), CHICAGO. NARROW ROMAN BRICK WAS A WRIGHT TRADE-MARK, BUT THE ENTRY'S LIMESTONE DETAILING BEARS A EUROPEAN TOUCH.

JANUARY

S	M	T	W	T	F	S	S	M	T	W	T	F	S	S	M	T	W	T	F	S	S	M	T	W	T	F	S	S	M	T
1	2	3	4	5	6	7	8	9	10	11	12	13	14	15	16	17	18	19	20	21	22	23	24	25	26	27	28	29	30	31

MONDAY

23

◑ TUESDAY

24

WEDNESDAY

25

THURSDAY

26

FRIDAY

27

SATURDAY

28

SUNDAY

29

PEARCE HOUSE (1950), BRADBURY, CALIFORNIA. WAXED RED CONCRETE FLOORS INCISED WITH GEOMETRIC GRIDS MAKE WRIGHT'S USONIAN HOUSES GLOW.

JANUARY

S	M	T	W	T	F	S	S	M	T	W	T	F	S	S	M	T	W	T	F	S	S	M	T	W	T	F	S	S	M	T
1	2	3	4	5	6	7	8	9	10	11	12	13	14	15	16	17	18	19	20	21	22	23	24	25	26	27	28	29	30	31

JANUARY □ FEBRUARY

MONDAY ●

30

TUESDAY

31

WEDNESDAY

1

THURSDAY

2

FRIDAY

3

SATURDAY

4

SUNDAY

5

BRADLEY HOUSE (1900), KANKAKEE, ILLINOIS. CUSTOM-MADE DINING CHAIRS REFLECTED THE ARCHITECTURE AND HELPED LAUNCH THE PRAIRIE STYLE.

FEBRUARY

W	T	F	S	S	M	T	W	T	F	S	S	M	T	W	T	F	S	S	M	T	W	T	F	S	S	M	T
1	2	3	4	5	6	7	8	9	10	11	12	13	14	15	16	17	18	19	20	21	22	23	24	25	26	27	28

MONDAY

6

◑ TUESDAY

7

WEDNESDAY

8

THURSDAY

9

FRIDAY

10

SATURDAY

11

LINCOLN'S BIRTHDAY

SUNDAY

12

WALKER HOUSE (1948), CARMEL, CALIFORNIA. A "NATURAL MELODY" RESULTED, SAID WRIGHT, WHERE THE HOUSE JOINED THE SEA'S LONG, WHITE SURF LINES.

FEBRUARY

W	T	F	S	S	M	T	W	T	F	S	S	M	T	W	T	F	S	S	M	T	W	T	F	S	S	M	T
1	2	3	4	5	6	7	8	9	10	11	12	13	14	15	16	17	18	19	20	21	22	23	24	25	26	27	28

FEBRUARY

MONDAY

13

TUESDAY   VALENTINE'S DAY

14

WEDNESDAY ○

15

THURSDAY

16

FRIDAY

17

SATURDAY

18

SUNDAY

19

FALLINGWATER (1935), MILL RUN, PENNSYLVANIA. VERTICALS AND HORIZONTALS INTERSECT DECISIVELY IN THE BUILT-IN CLOSETS OF THE MAIN BEDROOM.

FEBRUARY

W	T	F	S	S	M	T	W	T	F	S	S	M	T	W	T	F	S	S	M	T	W	T	F	S	S	M	T
1	2	3	4	5	6	7	8	9	10	11	12	13	14	15	16	17	18	19	20	21	22	23	24	25	26	27	28

FEBRUARY

PRESIDENTS' DAY

MONDAY

20

TUESDAY

21

WASHINGTON'S BIRTHDAY

◑ WEDNESDAY

22

THURSDAY

23

FRIDAY

24

SATURDAY

25

SUNDAY

26

FALLINGWATER (1935), MILL RUN, PENNSYLVANIA. TUCKED INTO A GLASSY CORNER, THE MASTER BATH BRINGS THE OUTSIDE IN WITH SMALL PLANTER BOXES.

FEBRUARY

W	T	F	S	S	M	T	W	T	F	S	S	M	T	W	T	F	S	S	M	T	W	T	F	S	S	M	T
1	2	3	4	5	6	7	8	9	10	11	12	13	14	15	16	17	18	19	20	21	22	23	24	25	26	27	28

FEBRUARY □ MARCH

MONDAY

27

TUESDAY

28

WEDNESDAY ●   ASH WEDNESDAY

1

THURSDAY

2

FRIDAY

3

SATURDAY

4

SUNDAY

5

FALLINGWATER (1935), MILL RUN, PENNSYLVANIA. LIKE THE PROW OF A GREAT
CONCRETE SHIP, FALLINGWATER'S BALCONIES SLICE THROUGH BEAR RUN.

MARCH

W	T	F	S	S	M	T	W	T	F	S	S	M	T	W	T	F	S	S	M	T	W	T	F	S	S	M	T	W	T	F
1	2	3	4	5	6	7	8	9	10	11	12	13	14	15	16	17	18	19	20	21	22	23	24	25	26	27	28	29	30	31

MONDAY
6

TUESDAY
7

WEDNESDAY
8

 THURSDAY
9

FRIDAY
10

SATURDAY
11

SUNDAY
12

HOLLYHOCK HOUSE (1917), HOLLYWOOD. USING GLASS AND CONCRETE, WRIGHT GAVE ALINE BARNSDALL VARIED BOUQUETS OF THE HOLLYHOCKS SHE LOVED.

MARCH

W	T	F	S	S	M	T	W	T	F	S	S	M	T	W	T	F	S	S	M	T	W	T	F	S	S	M	T	W	T	F
1	2	3	4	5	6	7	8	9	10	11	12	13	14	15	16	17	18	19	20	21	22	23	24	25	26	27	28	29	30	31

MARCH

MONDAY

13

TUESDAY

14

WEDNESDAY

15

THURSDAY

16

FRIDAY ○   ST. PATRICK'S DAY

17

SATURDAY

18

SUNDAY

19

HOLLYHOCK HOUSE (1917), HOLLYWOOD. CAST-CONCRETE STALKS OF HOLLY HOCK FLOWERS STAND TALL TO SERVE AS COLUMNS AND DECORATIVE FRIEZES.

MARCH

W	T	F	S	S	M	T	W	T	F	S	S	M	T	W	T	F	S	S	M	T	W	T	F	S	S	M	T	W	T	F
1	2	3	4	5	6	7	8	9	10	11	12	13	14	15	16	17	18	19	20	21	22	23	24	25	26	27	28	29	30	31

MONDAY

20

VERNAL EQUINOX

TUESDAY

21

WEDNESDAY

22

◑ THURSDAY

23

FRIDAY

24

SATURDAY

25

SUNDAY

26

ROBERT LLEWELLYN WRIGHT HOUSE (1953), BETHESDA, MARYLAND. IN THIS UN-
USUAL HEMICYCLE HOUSE, A SQUARED-UP NOOK LIKE THIS IS RARE.

MARCH

W	T	F	S	S	M	T	W	T	F	S	S	M	T	W	T	F	S	S	M	T	W	T	F	S	S	M	T	W	T	F
1	2	3	4	5	6	7	8	9	10	11	12	13	14	15	16	17	18	19	20	21	22	23	24	25	26	27	28	29	30	31

MARCH □ APRIL

MONDAY

27

TUESDAY

28

WEDNESDAY

29

THURSDAY

30

FRIDAY ●

31

SATURDAY

1

SUNDAY

2

ADAMS HOUSE (1905), HIGHLAND PARK, ILLINOIS. SHELTERING ROOFS WITH BROAD, PROTECTIVE EAVES CLEARLY OWE THEIR ORIGINS TO THE PRAIRIE.

APRIL

S	S	M	T	W	T ·F	S	S	M	T	W	T	F	S	S	M	T	W	T	F	S	S	M	T	W	T	F	S	S
1	2	3	4	5	6	7	8	9	10	11	12	13	14	15	16	17	18	19	20	21	22	23	24	25	26	27	28	29	30

MONDAY

3

TUESDAY

4

WEDNESDAY

5

THURSDAY

6

FRIDAY

7

◐ SATURDAY

8

PALM SUNDAY

SUNDAY

9

MAY HOUSE (1908), GRAND RAPIDS, MICHIGAN. THE FAMILY DINED SURROUNDED
BY GARDENS—ONE REAL, THE OTHER A GOLDEN FICTION ON THE DIVIDING WALL.

APRIL
S	S	M	T	W	T	F	S	S	M	T	W	T	F	S	S	M	T	W	T	F	S	S	M	T	W	T	F	S	S
1	2	3	4	5	6	7	8	9	10	11	12	13	14	15	16	17	18	19	20	21	22	23	24	25	26	27	28	29	30

APRIL

MONDAY

10

TUESDAY

11

WEDNESDAY

12

THURSDAY

13

FRIDAY   GOOD FRIDAY / PASSOVER (SUNDOWN)

14

SATURDAY ○

15

SUNDAY   EASTER SUNDAY

16

MAY HOUSE (1908), GRAND RAPIDS, MICHIGAN. ABSTRACTED LEAF PATTERNS APPEAR
UNDERFOOT, IN THE CARPETS, AS WELL AS THROUGHOUT THE PRAIRIE STYLE HOUSE.

APRIL

S	S	M	T	W	T	F	S	S	M	T	W	T	F	S	S	M	T	W	T	F	S	S	M	T	W	T	F	S	S
1	2	3	4	5	6	7	8	9	10	11	12	13	14	15	16	17	18	19	20	21	22	23	24	25	26	27	28	29	30

EASTER MONDAY (CANADA)

MONDAY

17

TUESDAY

18

WEDNESDAY

19

THURSDAY

20

FRIDAY

21

EARTH DAY

◗ SATURDAY

22

SUNDAY

23

TALIESIN (1911–59), SPRING GREEN, WISCONSIN. WRIGHT CHOSE THE WELSH WORD TALIESIN, MEANING "SHINING BROW," FOR HIS HILLSIDE HOME.

APRIL

S	M	T	W	T	F	S	S	M	T	W	T	F	S	S	M	T	W	T	F	S	S	M	T	W	T	F	S	S
1	2	3	4	5	6	7	8	9	10	11	12	13	14	15	16	17	18	19	20	21	22	23	24	25	26	27	28	29	30

APRIL

MONDAY

24

TUESDAY

25

WEDNESDAY

26

THURSDAY

27

FRIDAY

28

SATURDAY ●

29

SUNDAY

30

TALIESIN (1911–59), SPRING GREEN, WISCONSIN. AN ANCIENT BELL CALLED THE WRIGHTS AND THE APPRENTICES TO THE TEA CIRCLE EACH AFTERNOON.

APRIL

S	S	M	T	W	T	F	S	S	M	T	W	T	F	S	S	M	T	W	T	F	S	S	M	T	W	T	F	S	S
1	2	3	4	5	6	7	8	9	10	11	12	13	14	15	16	17	18	19	20	21	22	23	24	25	26	27	28	29	30

MAY

MONDAY

1

TUESDAY

2

WEDNESDAY

3

THURSDAY

4

CINCO DE MAYO   FRIDAY

5

SATURDAY

6

◗ SUNDAY

7

TALIESIN (1911–59), SPRING GREEN, WISCONSIN. LIMESTONE WALLS INSIDE AND
OUT WERE LAID IN ALTERNATING ROWS AS THEY CAME FROM THE QUARRY.

MAY
M T W T F S S M T W T F S S M T W T F S S M T W T F S S M T W
1 2 3 4 5 6 7 8 9 10 11 12 13 14 15 16 17 18 19 20 21 22 23 24 25 26 27 28 29 30 31

MAY

MONDAY

8

TUESDAY

9

WEDNESDAY

10

THURSDAY

11

FRIDAY

12

SATURDAY

13

SUNDAY ○   MOTHER'S DAY

14

ABLIN HOUSE (1958), BAKERSFIELD, CALIFORNIA. PERFORATED CONCRETE
BLOCKS DIRECT LIGHT INTO WHAT WRIGHT LIKED TO CALL THE "WORKSPACE."

MAY

M	T	W	T	F	S	S	M	T	W	T	F	S	S	M	T	W	T	F	S	S	M	T	W	T	F	S	S	M	T	W
1	2	3	4	5	6	7	8	9	10	11	12	13	14	15	16	17	18	19	20	21	22	23	24	25	26	27	28	29	30	31

MAY

MONDAY

15

TUESDAY

16

WEDNESDAY

17

THURSDAY

18

FRIDAY

19

ARMED FORCES DAY

SATURDAY

20

◑ SUNDAY

21

RAVINE BLUFFS (1915), GLENCOE, ILLINOIS. POURED CONCRETE SCULPTURES GUARD
THE ENTRANCE TO THIS SMALL DEVELOPMENT THAT WAS ONCE GRANDLY CONCEIVED.

MAY

M	T	W	T	F	S	S	M	T	W	T	F	S	S	M	T	W	T	F	S	S	M	T	W	T	F	S	S	M	T	W
1	2	3	4	5	6	7	8	9	10	11	12	13	14	15	16	17	18	19	20	21	22	23	24	25	26	27	28	29	30	31

MAY

MONDAY   VICTORIA DAY (CANADA)

22

TUESDAY

23

WEDNESDAY

24

THURSDAY

25

FRIDAY

26

SATURDAY

27

SUNDAY

28

DANA-THOMAS HOUSE (1904), SPRINGFIELD, ILLINOIS. NOT LONG OUT OF LOUIS SULLIVAN'S OFFICE, WRIGHT CREATED A PLASTER FRIEZE THAT WAS HIS OWN.

MAY

M	T	W	T	F	S	S	M	T	W	T	F	S	S	M	T	W	T	F	S	S	M	T	W	T	F	S	S	M	T	W
1	2	3	4	5	6	7	8	9	10	11	12	13	14	15	16	17	18	19	20	21	22	23	24	25	26	27	28	29	30	31

MEMORIAL DAY (OBSERVED)

● MONDAY

29

MEMORIAL DAY

TUESDAY

30

WEDNESDAY

31

THURSDAY

1

FRIDAY

2

SATURDAY

3

SUNDAY

4

MARIN COUNTY CIVIC CENTER (1957–72), SAN RAFAEL, CALIFORNIA. THE CENTER'S LANDMARK PYLON HOVERS BEYOND THE ATRIUM IN THE HALL OF JUSTICE.

JUNE

T	F	S	S	M	T	W	T	F	S	S	M	T	W	T	F	S	S	M	T	W	T	F	S	S	M	T	W	T	F
1	2	3	4	5	6	7	8	9	10	11	12	13	14	15	16	17	18	19	20	21	22	23	24	25	26	27	28	29	30

JUNE

MONDAY

5

TUESDAY ◐

6

WEDNESDAY

7

THURSDAY   FRANK LLOYD WRIGHT BORN, 1867

8

FRIDAY

9

SATURDAY

10

SUNDAY

11

TALIESIN (1911–59), SPRING GREEN, WISCONSIN. ALTHOUGH WRIGHT'S BUILD-
INGS NEEDED NO SIGNATURE, HE FOUND VARIOUS WAYS OF MARKING THEM.

JUNE

T	F	S	S	M	T	W	T	F	S	S	M	T	W	T	F	S	S	M	T	W	T	F	S	S	M	T	W	T	F
1	2	3	4	5	6	7	8	9	10	11	12	13	14	15	16	17	18	19	20	21	22	23	24	25	26	27	28	29	30

FRANK
LLOYD
WRIGHT

ARCHITECT

MONDAY

12

○ TUESDAY

13

FLAG DAY

WEDNESDAY

14

THURSDAY

15

FRIDAY

16

SATURDAY

17

FATHER'S DAY

SUNDAY

18

LA MINIATURA (1923), PASADENA, CALIFORNIA. THE FIRST OF FOUR TEX-
TILE-BLOCK DESIGNS, ALICE MILLARD'S HOUSE WAS THE MOST ROMANTIC.

JUNE

T	F	S	S	M	T	W	T	F	S	S	M	T	W	T	F	S	S	M	T	W	T	F	S	S	M	T	W	T	F
1	2	3	4	5	6	7	8	9	10	11	12	13	14	15	16	17	18	19	20	21	22	23	24	25	26	27	28	29	30

JUNE

19

TUESDAY

20

WEDNESDAY   SUMMER SOLSTICE

21

THURSDAY

22

FRIDAY

23

SATURDAY

24

SUNDAY

25

TALIESIN WEST (1937), SCOTTSDALE, ARIZONA. WITH BOULDERS FROM THE DESERT AND FORMS THAT MIMIC THE HILLS, TALIESIN WEST IS ONE WITH ITS SITE.

JUNE

T	F	S	S	M	T	W	T	F	S	S	M	T	W	T	F	S	S	M	T	W	T	F	S	S	M	T	W	T	F
1	2	3	4	5	6	7	8	9	10	11	12	13	14	15	16	17	18	19	20	21	22	23	24	25	26	27	28	29	30

MONDAY

26

TUESDAY

27

● WEDNESDAY

28

THURSDAY

29

FRIDAY

30

CANADA DAY (CANADA)   SATURDAY

1

SUNDAY

2

TALIESIN WEST (1937), SCOTTSDALE, ARIZONA. A SPIRAL SIGN IN CHEROKEE
RED, ONE OF WRIGHT'S FAVORITE ACCENT COLORS, PROVIDES A WARM WELCOME.

JULY

S	S	M	T	W	T	F	S	S	M	T	W	T	F	S	S	M	T	W	T	F	S	S	M	T	W	T	F	S	S	M
1	2	3	4	5	6	7	8	9	10	11	12	13	14	15	16	17	18	19	20	21	22	23	24	25	26	27	28	29	30	31

JULY

MONDAY   CANADA DAY (OBSERVED) (CANADA)

3

TUESDAY   INDEPENDENCE DAY

4

WEDNESDAY ◑

5

THURSDAY

6

FRIDAY

7

SATURDAY

8

SUNDAY

9

FAWCETT HOUSE (1955), LOS BANOS, CALIFORNIA. STEPPED CONCRETE WALLS OF
THE HOUSE AND ENCLOSURE ARE MIRRORED IN STAIRS LEADING TO THE POOL.

JULY
S S M T W T F S S M T W T F S S M T W T F S S M T W T F S S M
1 2 3 4 5 6 7 8 9 10 11 12 13 14 15 16 17 18 19 20 21 22 23 24 25 26 27 28 29 30 31

JULY

MONDAY

10

TUESDAY

11

○ WEDNESDAY

12

THURSDAY

13

FRIDAY

14

SATURDAY

15

SUNDAY

16

GORDON HOUSE (1964), AURORA, OREGON. PERFORATED LIGHT SCREENS OPEN
THIS CONCRETE-BLOCK HOUSE TO VIEWS OF THE WILLAMETTE RIVER NEARBY.

JULY

S S M T W T F S S M T W T F S S M T W T F S S M T W T F S S M
1 2 3 4 5 6 7 8 9 10 11 12 13 14 15 16 17 18 19 20 21 22 23 24 25 26 27 28 29 30 31

JULY

MONDAY

17

TUESDAY

18

WEDNESDAY ◑

19

THURSDAY

20

FRIDAY

21

SATURDAY

22

SUNDAY

23

ENNIS HOUSE (1923), LOS ANGELES. LIKE A PRE-COLUMBIAN TEMPLE SCULPTED FROM THE HILLS, THE ENNIS HOUSE DISPLAYS ITS OWN UNIQUE BLOCK PATTERN.

JULY

S	S	M	T	W	T	F	S	S	M	T	W	T	F	S	S	M	T	W	T	F	S	S	M	T	W	T	F	S	S	M
1	2	3	4	5	6	7	8	9	10	11	12	13	14	15	16	17	18	19	20	21	22	23	24	25	26	27	28	29	30	31

MONDAY

24

TUESDAY

25

WEDNESDAY

26

● THURSDAY

27

FRIDAY

28

SATURDAY

29

SUNDAY

30

ENNIS HOUSE (1923), LOS ANGELES. WISTERIA IS A LEITMOTIF HERE, FROM SPARK-
LING ART GLASS WINDOWS TO A GOLDEN MOSAIC CROWN OVER A FIREPLACE.

JULY

S	S	M	T	W	T	F	S	S	M	T	W	T	F	S	S	M	T	W	T	F	S	S	M	T	W	T	F	S	S	M
1	2	3	4	5	6	7	8	9	10	11	12	13	14	15	16	17	18	19	20	21	22	23	24	25	26	27	28	29	30	31

JULY □ AUGUST

MONDAY

31

TUESDAY

1

WEDNESDAY

2

THURSDAY

3

FRIDAY ◐

4

SATURDAY

5

SUNDAY

6

HOME AND STUDIO (1889–98), OAK PARK, ILLINOIS. VISITORS TO WRIGHT'S STUDIO
WERE GREETED WITH BOLD PLANTERS, SCULPTURES, AND A MAZE OF SHAPES.

AUGUST

T	W	T	F	S	S	M	T	W	T	F	S	S	M	T	W	T	F	S	S	M	T	W	T	F	S	S	M	T	W	T
1	2	3	4	5	6	7	8	9	10	11	12	13	14	15	16	17	18	19	20	21	22	23	24	25	26	27	28	29	30	31

AUGUST

7

TUESDAY

8

WEDNESDAY

9

○ THURSDAY

10

FRIDAY

11

SATURDAY

12

SUNDAY

13

MAY HOUSE (1908), GRAND RAPIDS, MICHIGAN. STRATEGICALLY PLACED WIN-
DOWS AND SKYLIGHTS PULL NEEDED SUN INTO THIS NORTHERN HOUSE.

AUGUST

T	W	T	F	S	S	M	T	W	T	F	S	S	M	T	W	T	F	S	S	M	T	W	T	F	S	S	M	T	W	T
1	2	3	4	5	6	7	8	9	10	11	12	13	14	15	16	17	18	19	20	21	22	23	24	25	26	27	28	29	30	31

AUGUST

MONDAY

14

TUESDAY

15

WEDNESDAY

16

THURSDAY

17

FRIDAY ◑

18

SATURDAY

19

SUNDAY

20

MAY HOUSE (1908), GRAND RAPIDS, MICHIGAN. GEOMETRY REIGNS AS SQUARE PATTERNS IN THE COPPER ORNAMENT REPEAT THEMSELVES IN THE PAVING BLOCKS.

AUGUST

T	W	T	F	S	S	M	T	W	T	F	S	S	M	T	W	T	F	S	S	M	T	W	T	F	S	S	M	T	W	T
1	2	3	4	5	6	7	8	9	10	11	12	13	14	15	16	17	18	19	20	21	22	23	24	25	26	27	28	29	30	31

MONDAY

21

TUESDAY

22

WEDNESDAY

23

THURSDAY

24

FRIDAY

25

● SATURDAY

26

SUNDAY

27

UNITY TEMPLE (1904), OAK PARK, ILLINOIS. FOR WRIGHT, UNITY TEMPLE WAS
WHERE THE SPACE WITHIN FIRST BECAME THE REALITY OF THE BUILDING.

AUGUST

T	W	T	F	S	S	M	T	W	T	F	S	S	M	T	W	T	F	S	S	M	T	W	T	F	S	S	M	T	W	T
1	2	3	4	5	6	7	8	9	10	11	12	13	14	15	16	17	18	19	20	21	22	23	24	25	26	27	28	29	30	31

AUGUST □ SEPTEMBER

MONDAY

28

TUESDAY

29

WEDNESDAY

30

THURSDAY

31

FRIDAY

1

SATURDAY ◗

2

SUNDAY

3

BAZETT HOUSE (1939), HILLSBOROUGH, CALIFORNIA. FRENCH DOORS, CLERE-STORY CUTOUTS, AND RED CONCRETE FLOORS MARK THIS AS A USONIAN DESIGN.

SEPTEMBER

F	S	S	M	T	W	T	F	S	S	M	T	W	T	F	S	S	M	T	W	T	F	S	S	M	T	W	T	F	S
1	2	3	4	5	6	7	8	9	10	11	12	13	14	15	16	17	18	19	20	21	22	23	24	25	26	27	28	29	30

SEPTEMBER

LABOR DAY

MONDAY

4

TUESDAY

5

WEDNESDAY

6

THURSDAY

7

FRIDAY

8

○ SATURDAY

9

SUNDAY

10

BOOMER HOUSE (1953), PHOENIX. THE GRID OF THIS COMPACT RESIDENCE FORMS A PARALLELOGRAM, MAKING ITS BEDROOM BALCONY JUT OUT OVER THE FIRST FLOOR.

SEPTEMBER

F	S	S	M	T	W	T	F	S	S	M	T	W	T	F	S	S	M	T	W	T	F	S	S	M	T	W	T	F	S
1	2	3	4	5	6	7	8	9	10	11	12	13	14	15	16	17	18	19	20	21	22	23	24	25	26	27	28	29	30

SEPTEMBER

MONDAY

11

TUESDAY

12

WEDNESDAY

13

THURSDAY

14

FRIDAY

15

SATURDAY ◑

16

SUNDAY

17

STORER HOUSE (1923), HOLLYWOOD. TURNED UPSIDE DOWN, THE LIVING ROOM IS ON THE TOP FLOOR HERE. IT OPENS ONTO AN EXPANSIVE, LEAFY TERRACE.

SEPTEMBER

F	S	S	M	T	W	T	F	S	S	M	T	W	T	F	S	S	M	T	W	T	F	S	S	M	T	W	T	F	S
1	2	3	4	5	6	7	8	9	10	11	12	13	14	15	16	17	18	19	20	21	22	23	24	25	26	27	28	29	30

SEPTEMBER

MONDAY

18

TUESDAY

19

WEDNESDAY

20

THURSDAY

21

FRIDAY

22

AUTUMNAL EQUINOX

SATURDAY

23

ROSH HASHANAH (SUNDOWN)

● SUNDAY

24

BROWN HOUSE (1949), KALAMAZOO, MICHIGAN. PLAYING WATER AGAINST FIRE, WRIGHT SURROUNDED THIS EXTRA-WIDE HEARTH WITH A FLOWER-FILLED POOL.

SEPTEMBER

F	S	S	M	T	W	T	F	S	S	M	T	W	T	F	S	S	M	T	W	T	F	S	S	M	T	W	T	F	S
1	2	3	4	5	6	7	8	9	10	11	12	13	14	15	16	17	18	19	20	21	22	23	24	25	26	27	28	29	30

SEPTEMBER ☐ OCTOBER

MONDAY

25

TUESDAY

26

WEDNESDAY

27

THURSDAY

28

FRIDAY

29

SATURDAY

30

SUNDAY ◑

1

STURGES HOUSE (1939), BRENTWOOD, CALIFORNIA. SOARING OUT FROM A STEEP HILLSIDE PERCH, THE WRAPAROUND DECK MIGHT AS WELL BE A TREE HOUSE.

OCTOBER
S	M	T	W	T	F	S	S	M	T	W	T	F	S	S	M	T	W	T	F	S	S	M	T	W	T	F	S	S	M	T
1	2	3	4	5	6	7	8	9	10	11	12	13	14	15	16	17	18	19	20	21	22	23	24	25	26	27	28	29	30	31

OCTOBER

MONDAY

2

YOM KIPPUR (SUNDOWN)

TUESDAY

3

WEDNESDAY

4

THURSDAY

5

FRIDAY

6

SATURDAY

7

 SUNDAY

8

LITTLE HOUSE (1914), WAYZATA, MINNESOTA. THE MAJESTIC PRAIRIE STYLE LIVING
ROOM, DISASSEMBLED IN 1972, GRANDLY FRAMED A WINGED VICTORY SCULPTURE.

OCTOBER

S	M	T	W	T	F	S	S	M	T	W	T	F	S	S	M	T	W	T	F	S	S	M	T	W	T	F	S	S	M	T
1	2	3	4	5	6	7	8	9	10	11	12	13	14	15	16	17	18	19	20	21	22	23	24	25	26	27	28	29	30	31

OCTOBER

MONDAY   COLUMBUS DAY (OBSERVED) / THANKSGIVING DAY (CANADA)

9

TUESDAY

10

WEDNESDAY

11

THURSDAY   COLUMBUS DAY

12

FRIDAY

13

SATURDAY

14

SUNDAY

15

LITTLE HOUSE (1914), WAYZATA, MINNESOTA. NOW INSTALLED IN THE METRO POLITAN MUSEUM, THE FURNITURE GROUPINGS LEND HUMAN SCALE TO THE SPACE.

OCTOBER

S	M	T	W	T	F	S	S	M	T	W	T	F	S	S	M	T	W	T	F	S	S	M	T	W	T	F	S	S	M	T
1	2	3	4	5	6	7	8	9	10	11	12	13	14	15	16	17	18	19	20	21	22	23	24	25	26	27	28	29	30	31

OCTOBER

◐ MONDAY

16

TUESDAY

17

WEDNESDAY

18

THURSDAY

19

FRIDAY

20

SATURDAY

21

SUNDAY

22

BOYNTON HOUSE (1908), ROCHESTER, NEW YORK. AN EXTRAORDINARY DINING ROOM WAS SERVED FROM THIS KITCHEN, WHICH LOOKS ALMOST AS IT DID IN 1908.

OCTOBER

S	M	T	W	T	F	S	S	M	T	W	T	F	S	S	M	T	W	T	F	S	S	M	T	W	T	F	S	S	M	T
1	2	3	4	5	6	7	8	9	10	11	12	13	14	15	16	17	18	19	20	21	22	23	24	25	26	27	28	29	30	31

OCTOBER

MONDAY

23

TUESDAY ●   UNITED NATIONS DAY

24

WEDNESDAY

25

THURSDAY

26

FRIDAY

27

SATURDAY

28

SUNDAY

29

DANA-THOMAS HOUSE (1904), SPRINGFIELD, ILLINOIS. A CORRIDOR BECOMES A FOREST OF TREES SEPARATED BY SHIMMERING, TRANSPARENT FLOWERS.

OCTOBER

S	M	T	W	T	F	S	S	M	T	W	T	F	S	S	M	T	W	T	F	S	S	M	T	W	T	F	S	S	M	T
1	2	3	4	5	6	7	8	9	10	11	12	13	14	15	16	17	18	19	20	21	22	23	24	25	26	27	28	29	30	31

◗ MONDAY

30

HALLOWEEN

TUESDAY

31

WEDNESDAY

1

THURSDAY

2

FRIDAY

3

SATURDAY

4

SUNDAY

5

DANA-THOMAS HOUSE (1904), SPRINGFIELD, ILLINOIS. STYLIZED SUMAC LEAVES CASCADE THROUGHOUT. HERE THEY ARE JOINED BY ETHEREAL BUTTERFLIES.

NOVEMBER

W	T	F	S	S	M	T	W	T	F	S	S	M	T	W	T	F	S	S	M	T	W	T	F	S	S	M	T	W	T
1	2	3	4	5	6	7	8	9	10	11	12	13	14	15	16	17	18	19	20	21	22	23	24	25	26	27	28	29	30

NOVEMBER

MONDAY

6

TUESDAY ○   ELECTION DAY

7

WEDNESDAY

8

THURSDAY

9

FRIDAY

10

SATURDAY   VETERANS DAY / REMEMBRANCE DAY (CANADA)

11

SUNDAY

12

DANA-THOMAS HOUSE (1904), SPRINGFIELD, ILLINOIS. NO DETAIL WAS TOO SMALL. THIS WALL SCONCE IS ENLIVENED WITH WRIGHTIAN GEOMETRICS.

NOVEMBER

W	T	F	S	S	M	T	W	T	F	S	S	M	T	W	T	F	S	S	M	T	W	T	F	S	S	M	T	W	T
1	2	3	4	5	6	7	8	9	10	11	12	13	14	15	16	17	18	19	20	21	22	23	24	25	26	27	28	29	30

NOVEMBER

REMEMBRANCE DAY (OBSERVED) (CANADA)

MONDAY

13

TUESDAY

14

◑ WEDNESDAY

15

THURSDAY

16

FRIDAY

17

SATURDAY

18

SUNDAY

19

HOME AND STUDIO (1889–98), OAK PARK, ILLINOIS. FOR HIS OWN DINING ROOM
WRIGHT DESIGNED ONE OF HIS FIRST FREESTANDING PIECES OF FURNITURE.

NOVEMBER

W	T	F	S	S	M	T	W	T	F	S	S	M	T	W	T	F	S	S	M	T	W	T	F	S	S	M	T	W	T
1	2	3	4	5	6	7	8	9	10	11	12	13	14	15	16	17	18	19	20	21	22	23	24	25	26	27	28	29	30

NOVEMBER

MONDAY

20

TUESDAY

21

WEDNESDAY ●

22

THURSDAY   THANKSGIVING DAY

23

FRIDAY

24

SATURDAY

25

SUNDAY

26

HOME AND STUDIO (1889–98), OAK PARK, ILLINOIS. CHAIRS, TABLE, CABINETS, WINDOWS, LIGHTING — THE WHOLE FULFILLED WRIGHT'S VISION OF UNITY.

NOVEMBER

W	T	F	S	S	M	T	W	T	F	S	S	M	T	W	T	F	S	S	M	T	W	T	F	S	S	M	T	W	T
1	2	3	4	5	6	7	8	9	10	11	12	13	14	15	16	17	18	19	20	21	22	23	24	25	26	27	28	29	30

NOVEMBER ☐ DECEMBER

MONDAY

27

TUESDAY

28

◑ **WEDNESDAY**

29

THURSDAY

30

FRIDAY

1

SATURDAY

2

SUNDAY

3

HOME AND STUDIO (1889–98), OAK PARK, ILLINOIS. ALTHOUGH THE PATTERN IS
SIMPLIFIED, WRIGHT'S GENIUS WITH ART GLASS EMERGED EARLY IN HIS OWN HOME.

DECEMBER

F	S	S	M	T	W	T	F	S	S	M	T	W	T	F	S	S	M	T	W	T	F	S	S	M	T	W	T	F	S	S
1	2	3	4	5	6	7	8	9	10	11	12	13	14	15	16	17	18	19	20	21	22	23	24	25	26	27	28	29	30	31

DECEMBER

MONDAY

4

TUESDAY

5

WEDNESDAY

6

THURSDAY ○

7

FRIDAY

8

SATURDAY

9

SUNDAY

10

HOME AND STUDIO (1889–98), OAK PARK, ILLINOIS. WRIGHT MADE ROOM FOR A PIANO WHEREVER HE COULD, EVEN TUCKED INTO AN ALCOVE OF HIS PLAYROOM.

DECEMBER

F	S	S	M	T	W	T	F	S	S	M	T	W	T	F	S	S	M	T	W	T	F	S	S	M	T	W	T	F	S	S
1	2	3	4	5	6	7	8	9	10	11	12	13	14	15	16	17	18	19	20	21	22	23	24	25	26	27	28	29	30	31

DECEMBER

MONDAY

11

TUESDAY

12

WEDNESDAY

13

THURSDAY

14

◑ FRIDAY

15

SATURDAY

16

HANUKKAH (SUNDOWN)   SUNDAY

17

OBOLER HOUSE (1940–55), MALIBU, CALIFORNIA. AT THIS MOUNTAIN RETREAT
WOOD SIDING MAKES UPPER LEVELS SEEM TO FLOAT OVER A SOLID MASONRY BASE.

DECEMBER

F	S	S	M	T	W	T	F	S	S	M	T	W	T	F	S	S	M	T	W	T	F	S	S	M	T	W	T	F	S	S
1	2	3	4	5	6	7	8	9	10	11	12	13	14	15	16	17	18	19	20	21	22	23	24	25	26	27	28	29	30	31

DECEMBER

MONDAY

18

TUESDAY

19

WEDNESDAY

20

THURSDAY

21

FRIDAY ●   WINTER SOLSTICE

22

SATURDAY

23

SUNDAY

24

TRACY HOUSE (1955), SEATTLE. RECALLING AN ORIENTAL CHOP, WRIGHT SIGNED HIS BUILDINGS WITH A DISTINCTIVE RED CERAMIC SQUARE.

DECEMBER

F	S	S	M	T	W	T	F	S	S	M	T	W	T	F	S	S	M	T	W	T	F	S	S	M	T	W	T	F	S	S
1	2	3	4	5	6	7	8	9	10	11	12	13	14	15	16	17	18	19	20	21	22	23	24	25	26	27	28	29	30	31

DECEMBER

MONDAY

25

TUESDAY

26

WEDNESDAY

27

◗ THURSDAY

28

FRIDAY

29

SATURDAY

30

SUNDAY

31

STROMQUIST HOUSE (1958), BOUNTIFUL, UTAH. THE ROOF, SHELTERING A TERRACE, HELPS DEFINE THE PARALLELOGRAM GRID ON WHICH THE HOUSE IS BASED.

DECEMBER

F	S	S	M	T	W	T	F	S	S	M	T	W	T	F	S	S	M	T	W	T	F	S	S	M	T	W	T	F	S	S
1	2	3	4	5	6	7	8	9	10	11	12	13	14	15	16	17	18	19	20	21	22	23	24	25	26	27	28	29	30	31

1995

JANUARY
S	M	T	W	T	F	S
1	2	3	4	5	6	7
8	9	10	11	12	13	14
15	16	17	18	19	20	21
22	23	24	25	26	27	28
29	30	31				

FEBRUARY
S	M	T	W	T	F	S
			1	2	3	4
5	6	7	8	9	10	11
12	13	14	15	16	17	18
19	20	21	22	23	24	25
26	27	28				

MARCH
S	M	T	W	T	F	S
			1	2	3	4
5	6	7	8	9	10	11
12	13	14	15	16	17	18
19	20	21	22	23	24	25
26	27	28	29	30	31	

APRIL
S	M	T	W	T	F	S
						1
2	3	4	5	6	7	8
9	10	11	12	13	14	15
16	17	18	19	20	21	22
23	24	25	26	27	28	29
30						

MAY
S	M	T	W	T	F	S
	1	2	3	4	5	6
7	8	9	10	11	12	13
14	15	16	17	18	19	20
21	22	23	24	25	26	27
28	29	30	31			

JUNE
S	M	T	W	T	F	S
				1	2	3
4	5	6	7	8	9	10
11	12	13	14	15	16	17
18	19	20	21	22	23	24
25	26	27	28	29	30	

JULY
S	M	T	W	T	F	S
						1
2	3	4	5	6	7	8
9	10	11	12	13	14	15
16	17	18	19	20	21	22
23	24	25	26	27	28	29
30	31					

AUGUST
S	M	T	W	T	F	S
		1	2	3	4	5
6	7	8	9	10	11	12
13	14	15	16	17	18	19
20	21	22	23	24	25	26
27	28	29	30	31		

SEPTEMBER
S	M	T	W	T	F	S
					1	2
3	4	5	6	7	8	9
10	11	12	13	14	15	16
17	18	19	20	21	22	23
24	25	26	27	28	29	30

OCTOBER
S	M	T	W	T	F	S
1	2	3	4	5	6	7
8	9	10	11	12	13	14
15	16	17	18	19	20	21
22	23	24	25	26	27	28
29	30	31				

NOVEMBER
S	M	T	W	T	F	S
			1	2	3	4
5	6	7	8	9	10	11
12	13	14	15	16	17	18
19	20	21	22	23	24	25
26	27	28	29	30		

DECEMBER
S	M	T	W	T	F	S
					1	2
3	4	5	6	7	8	9
10	11	12	13	14	15	16
17	18	19	20	21	22	23
24	25	26	27	28	29	30
31						

1996

JANUARY
S	M	T	W	T	F	S
	1	2	3	4	5	6
7	8	9	10	11	12	13
14	15	16	17	18	19	20
21	22	23	24	25	26	27
28	29	30	31			

FEBRUARY
S	M	T	W	T	F	S
				1	2	3
4	5	6	7	8	9	10
11	12	13	14	15	16	17
18	19	20	21	22	23	24
25	26	27	28	29		

MARCH
S	M	T	W	T	F	S
					1	2
3	4	5	6	7	8	9
10	11	12	13	14	15	16
17	18	19	20	21	22	23
24	25	26	27	28	29	30
31						

APRIL
S	M	T	W	T	F	S
	1	2	3	4	5	6
7	8	9	10	11	12	13
14	15	16	17	18	19	20
21	22	23	24	25	26	27
28	29	30				

MAY
S	M	T	W	T	F	S
			1	2	3	4
5	6	7	8	9	10	11
12	13	14	15	16	17	18
19	20	21	22	23	24	25
26	27	28	29	30	31	

JUNE
S	M	T	W	T	F	S
						1
2	3	4	5	6	7	8
9	10	11	12	13	14	15
16	17	18	19	20	21	22
23	24	25	26	27	28	29
30						

JULY
S	M	T	W	T	F	S
	1	2	3	4	5	6
7	8	9	10	11	12	13
14	15	16	17	18	19	20
21	22	23	24	25	26	27
28	29	30	31			

AUGUST
S	M	T	W	T	F	S
				1	2	3
4	5	6	7	8	9	10
11	12	13	14	15	16	17
18	19	20	21	22	23	24
25	26	27	28	29	30	31

SEPTEMBER
S	M	T	W	T	F	S
1	2	3	4	5	6	7
8	9	10	11	12	13	14
15	16	17	18	19	20	21
22	23	24	25	26	27	28
29	30					

OCTOBER
S	M	T	W	T	F	S
		1	2	3	4	5
6	7	8	9	10	11	12
13	14	15	16	17	18	19
20	21	22	23	24	25	26
27	28	29	30	31		

NOVEMBER
S	M	T	W	T	F	S
					1	2
3	4	5	6	7	8	9
10	11	12	13	14	15	16
17	18	19	20	21	22	23
24	25	26	27	28	29	30

DECEMBER
S	M	T	W	T	F	S
1	2	3	4	5	6	7
8	9	10	11	12	13	14
15	16	17	18	19	20	21
22	23	24	25	26	27	28
29	30	31				

CATALOG NO. 95205

AN ARCHETYPE PRESS CALENDAR

PUBLISHED BY POMEGRANATE CALENDARS & BOOKS
BOX 6099, ROHNERT PARK, CALIFORNIA 94927

ISBN-1-56640-909-8

AVAILABLE IN CANADA FROM FIREFLY BOOKS, LTD.
250 SPARKS AVENUE, WILLOWDALE, ONTARIO M2H 2S4

AVAILABLE IN THE U.K. AND MAINLAND EUROPE FROM POMEGRANATE EUROPE, LTD.
P.O. BOX 4, MALDON, ESSEX CM9 7XD, ENGLAND

AVAILABLE IN AUSTRALIA FROM BOOBOOK PUBLICATIONS PTY. LTD.
P.O. BOX 163 OR FREEPOST 1, TEA GARDENS 2324

AVAILABLE IN NEW ZEALAND FROM RANDY HORWOOD, LTD.
P.O. BOX 100–055 NORTH SHORE MAIL CENTRE OR 46 ELLICE ROAD NO. 14,
GLENFIELD, AUCKLAND

AVAILABLE IN ASIA (INCLUDING THE MIDDLE EAST), AFRICA, AND LATIN AMERICA
FROM POMEGRANATE PACIFIC, LTD.
113 BABCOMBE DRIVE, THORNHILL, ONTARIO L3T 1M9, CANADA

PRODUCED BY ARCHETYPE PRESS, INC., WASHINGTON, D.C.
DIANE MADDEX, PROJECT DIRECTOR
MARC ALAIN MEADOWS AND ROBERT L. WISER, ART DIRECTORS

ADAPTED FROM THE BOOK **THE WRIGHT STYLE**
BY CARLA LIND (SIMON & SCHUSTER, 1992)

TEXT COMPOSED IN GILL SANS, WITH DISPLAY TYPOGRAPHY IN PRAIRIE, A TYPEFACE
CREATED ESPECIALLY FOR **THE WRIGHT STYLE** BY ROBERT L. WISER OF ARCHETYPE PRESS

PRINTED IN KOREA

◑ FIRST QUARTER   ○ FULL MOON   ◐ LAST QUARTER   ● NEW MOON